CW00544961

A Mouth-Watering Traeger Grill Smoker Cookbook

Step-by-step recipes cookbook with easy and detailed instructions, begin grill like a pitmaster

Adam Green

Copyright 2021 - All rights reserved.

The content contained within this book may not be reproduced, duplicated or transmitted without direct written permission from the author or the publisher.

Under no circumstances will any blame or legal responsibility be held against the publisher, or author, for any damages, reparation, or monetary loss due to the information contained within this book. Either directly or indirectly.

Legal Notice:

This book is copyright protected. This book is only for personal use. You cannot amend, distribute, sell, use, quote or paraphrase any part, or the content within this book, without the consent of the author or publisher.

Disclaimer Notice:

Please note the information contained within this document is for educational and entertainment purposes only. All effort has been executed to present accurate, up to date, and reliable, complete information. No warranties of any kind are declared or implied. Readers acknowledge that the author is not engaging in the rendering of legal, financial, medical or professional advice. The content within this book has been derived from various sources. Please consult a licensed professional before attempting any techniques outlined in this book.

By reading this document, the reader agrees that under no circumstances is the author responsible for any losses, direct or indirect, which are incurred as a result of the use of information contained within this document, including, but not limited to, errors, omissions, or inaccuracies.

Table Of Contents

Introduction

Thank you very much for purchasing this cookbook.

For specific versions, the Traeger pellet grill will need you the best wood to get a smoky fire and automatically pumped into the barbecue to keep the fire burning. The results are remarkable. You can cook any type of meat, even fish, with these grills. I've seen baked cookies you wouldn't believe. This is a truly versatile outdoor barbecue. This wood pellet grill can offer you the effortless experience by ensuring your unique flavor to your recipes. Traeger wood pellet grills are designed to allow you to have a hands-free approach to grilling by letting one machine do the amount of work. The dishes I have proposed to you are simple and delicious, and thanks to the pellet grill they will take on an exceptional taste! Enjoy your meal!

Smoked Beef Recipes

1.   Reverse-Seared Steaks

Preparation time: 15 minutes

Cooking time: 1 or 2 hours

Servings: 4

Ingredients:

- 4 (4-ounces) sirloin steaks
- 2 tablespoons olive oil
- Salt
- Freshly ground black pepper
- 4 tablespoons butter

Directions:

1.   Pat the steaks dry with paper towels.

2.   Season liberally with salt and pepper on both sides.

3.   Preheat the oven to 225 °F. Heat a cast-iron or heavy-bottomed ovenproof skillet over medium-high heat.

4.   Add the olive oil and, when it ripples, add the steaks to the pan. Sear the steaks on all sides, 2-3 minutes per side.

5.   Remove the pan from the heat.

6.   Top the steaks with 2 tablespoons of butter for each steak.

7.   Place the pan in the preheated oven and cook until the centers of the steaks have a minimum internal temperature of about 135°F.

8.   Remove the steaks from the oven and cover with foil for about 2

9.   minutes. Remove from the pan and serve while hot.

Nutrition:

- **Energy (calories):** 1285 kcal

- **Protein:** 123.02 g

- **Fat:** 84.43 g

- **Carbohydrates:** 0.01 g

- **Calcium:** 164 mg

- **Magnesium:** 126 mg

- **Phosphorus:** 1156 mg

- **Iron:** 9.25 mg

2.   Dijon Corned Beef Brisket

Preparation time: 15 minutes

Cooking time: 5 hours

Servings: 4

Ingredients

- 1 (3 pounds / 1.4 kg) flat cut corned beef brisket

- fat cap at least one-fourth inch thick

- one-fourth cup Dijon mustard

- 1 bottle Traeger Apricot BBQ Sauce

Direction

1.   Preheat Traeger grill to 225 °F (110 °C)

2.   Cut the fat cap off the corned beef brisket in strips about ½-inch (1.2 cm) thick

3. Cook the corned beef brisket fat side up in the

4. Traeger at 225 °F (110 °C) until the internal temperature reaches 90 °F (32 °C)

5. Flip the corned beef brisket and continue to cook until internal temperature reaches 110 °F (43 °C)

6. Corned beef brisket is done when the internal temperature reaches 160 °F (71 °C)

7. Wrap in foil and place in a large pan

8. Pour the BBQ sauce over the meat and top with the mustard

9. Serve with mashed potatoes and vegetables of your choice

Nutrition:

- **Energy (calories):** 647 kcal

- **Protein:** 26.73 g

- **Fat:** 59.03 g

- **Carbohydrates:** 5.78 g

- **Calcium:** 55 mg

- **Magnesium:** 58 mg

- **Phosphorus:** 320 mg

- **Iron:** 3.37 mg

3.   Garlic-Parmesan Crusted Filet Mignon

Preparation time: 15 minutes

Cooking time: 10 minutes

Servings: 4

Ingredients

- 8 fillets mignon

- 2 teaspoons garlic salt

- 2 teaspoons black pepper

- 2 teaspoons salt

- 2 cups grated Parmesan cheese

- 8 garlic, minced

- 2 tablespoons Dijon mustard

Direction

1.   Season the fillets with garlic salt, pepper, and salt. Combine the cheese and minced garlic in a shallow bowl.

2.   When ready to cook, set Traeger temperature to High and preheat, lid closed for 15 minutes.

3.   Put the fillets on the grill and cook each side for 4 minutes. When done, spread the Dijon mustard onto the fillets, then dredge in the cheese-garlic mixture. Return the filletss to the grill and cook for an additional 1 to 2 minutes, or until the cheese melts.

4.   Cool for 5 minutes before serving.

Nutrition:

- **Energy (calories):** 962 kcal

- **Protein:** 72.46 g

- **Fat:** 69.24 g

- **Carbohydrates:** 8.8 g

- **Calcium:** 507 mg

- **Magnesium:** 83 mg

- **Phosphorus:** 869 mg

- **Iron:** 4.78 mg

4.   Coffee Rub Brisket

Preparation time: 15 minutes

Cooking time: 9 hours

Servings: 8

Ingredients

- 15 pounds (6.8 kg) whole packer brisket

- 1 and one-half cups water, divided

- 2 tablespoons Traeger Coffee Rub, divided

- 2 tablespoons salt, divided

Direction

1.   Trim excess fat from brisket; place in a 6- to 7-quart slow cooker. Add one-half cup of the water, 1 tablespoon of the rub, and 1 tablespoon of the salt; cover.

2.   Place a smoker over high heat. When cooker reaches 285 °F, reduce heat to low; cook 7–9 hours or until fork-tender, adding more water if necessary, to keep beef covered.

3.   Cut brisket across the grain into ¼-inch (0.6-cm) slices. Keep warm.

4.   Place cooking liquid in a large saucepan. Add remaining water and remaining 1 tablespoon rub and 1 tablespoon salt; cook over medium heat 15 minutes or until liquid is reduced to a syrupy consistency. Serve with beef slices.

Nutrition

- **Energy (calories):** 1123 kcal

- **Protein:** 182.61 g

- **Fat:** 43.46 g

- **Carbohydrates:** 0 g

- **Calcium:** 115 mg

- **Magnesium:** 205 mg

- **Phosphorus:** 1888 mg

- **Iron:** 17.54 mg

- **Cholesterol:** 570 mg

Smoke Pork Recipes

5.   Spicy Pork Chops

Preparation time: 4 hours

Cooking time: 10-15 minutes

Servings: 4

Ingredients:

- 1 tbsp. olive oil

- 2 cloves garlic, crushed and minced

- 1 tbsp. cayenne pepper

- One-half tsp. hot sauce

- One-fourth cup lime juice

- 2 tsp. ground cumin

- 1 tsp. ground cinnamon

- 4 pork chops

- Lettuce

Directions:

1.   Mix the olive oil, garlic, cayenne pepper, hot sauce, lime juice, cumin, and cinnamon.

2.   Pour the mixture into a re-sealable plastic bag. Place the pork chops inside. Seal and turn to coat evenly. Chill in the refrigerator for 4 hours. Grill for 10 to 15 minutes, flipping occasionally.

Nutrition:

- **Energy (calories):** 418 kcal

- **Protein:** 44.31 g

- **Fat:** 21.81 g

- **Carbohydrates:** 12.95 g

- **Calcium:** 155 mg

- **Magnesium:** 83 mg

- **Phosphorus:** 448 mg

- **Iron:** 5.3 mg

- **Cholesterol:** 132 mg

- **Fiber:** 3.9 g

- **Sugars total:** 3.59 g

6.   Foolproof Baby Back Ribs

Preparation time: 4 hours

Cooking time: 6 hours

Servings: 4

Ingredients:

- 2 full slabs baby back ribs

- 1 cup mustard

- 1 cup All-Purpose Meat Rub

- 1 cup firmly packed brown sugar, divided

- 1 cup Perfection Spray and Mop Sauce, prepared in a spray bottle

- 1 cup Bluesy Competition BBQ Sauce

Direction:

1.   Heat grill. Coat ribs with rub then set aside.

2.   Add wood chunks and charcoal to grill. Place ribs on the grill, meaty side down.

3.   Coat mustard-coated ribs with rib rub. Cover grill and cook ribs for 5 hours at 325 degrees F (160 degrees C).

4.   Using tongs, slide ribs to the meaty side of the grill. Brush ribs with mop sauce and cooks for 1 hour.

5.   Remove ribs to a platter and brush ribs with half of the BBQ sauce. Allow ribs to rest 5 minutes before serving.

Nutrition:

- **Energy (calories):** 2113 kcal
- **Protein:** 166.77 g
- **Fat:** 134.41 g
- **Carbohydrates:** 61.68 g
- **Calcium:** 323 mg
- **Magnesium:** 214 mg
- **Phosphorus:** 1340 mg
- **Iron:** 17.47 mg
- **Cholesterol:** 546 mg
- **Fiber:** 4.6 g
- **Sugars total:** 27.79 g

7.   Spicy Candied Bacon

Preparation time: 15 minutes

Cooking time: 2 hours

Servings: 6-8

Ingredients:

- 2 pounds thick-cut bacon (about 24 slices)

- 1 cup firmly packed brown sugar

- 2 to 4 teaspoons ground cayenne pepper, depending on heat preference

- One-half cup maple syrup, divided

Direction:

1.   Arrange the bacon in a single layer on the baking sheet. Set aside a spoonful of brown sugar for a dipping sauce.

2.   Preheat oven to 350 °F/180 °C. Bake bacon for 15 minutes.

3.   After 15 minutes, brush the bacon with about half of the maple syrup and sprinkle with half the brown sugar. Refrigerate for 30 minutes.

4.   Brush with half the maple syrup. Sprinkle with half the brown sugar (less than the first time) and another 1 to 2 teaspoons cayenne pepper.

5.   Bake for 45 to 60 minutes. Longer baking will yield crispier bacon. Stir the bacon every 15 minutes or so. Serve with the remaining maple syrup.

Nutrition:

- **Energy (calories):** 566 kcal
- **Protein:** 14.44 g
- **Fat:** 44.57 g
- **Carbohydrates:** 27.68 g
- **Calcium:** 27 mg
- **Magnesium:** 21 mg
- **Phosphorus:** 210 mg
- **Iron:** 0.64 mg
- **Potassium:** 654 mg
- **Fiber:** 0.2 g
- **Sugars total:** 25.64 g

8. Chipotle Mustard–Slathered Ham

Preparation time: 10 minutes

Cooking time: 5 hours

Servings: 10-12

Ingredients:

- 1 (10- to 12-pounds) whole bone-in ham, fully cooked

- 1 cup Chipotle Mustard Slathering Sauce, divided

- One-fourth cup firmly packed brown sugar

- 2 teaspoons freshly ground black pepper

- 2 teaspoons ground cinnamon

Direction:

1.   Preheat the Traeger grill to 325 °F. Slather ham with ¼ cup Chipotle Mustard Slathering Sauce. Wrap ham tightly in foil. Bake ham for 5 hours.

2.   When the ham is almost done, combine brown sugar, pepper, and cinnamon in a small bowl. Unwrap ham and sprinkle with spice mixture. Return to oven for additional 30 minutes. Remove foil and bake for an additional 10 minutes to crisp up the skin.

3.   Serve with remaining Chipotle Mustard Slathering Sauce.

Nutrition:

- **Energy (calories):** 337 kcal

- **Protein:** 30.37 g

- **Fat:** 18.12 g

- **Carbohydrates:** 11.85 g

- **Calcium:** 38 mg

- **Magnesium:** 39 mg

- **Phosphorus:** 296 mg

- **Iron:** 1.77 mg

- **Potassium:** 436 mg

- **Cholesterol:** 101 mg

9.   Beyond basic Boston Butt

Preparation time: 10 minutes

Cooking time: 10 hours

Servings: 10-12

Ingredients:

- 1 (8- to 9-pounds) pork butt

- One-fourth cup mustard

- One-half cup All-Purpose Meat Rub

- 3 cups Perfection Spray and Mop Sauce, divided

- One-fourth cup salt

- 1 cup Bluesy Competition BBQ Sauce, for serving

Direction:

1.   Season the pork butt on all sides with salt and All-Purpose Meat Rub. Allow the meat to rest at room temperature for 1 hour.

2.   Fire up the grill for indirect cooking: Set burners to high

3.   Smoke the butt: Place the pork butt, fat-side down, on the

indirect-cooking side of the grill. Close the lid, and smoke the pork for 6 hours.

4.   Brush some mustard on the pork.

5.   To ensure a crusty, spray the fat cap of the pork with Perfection Spray and Mop Sauce 2 or 3 times.

6.   Cook the pork for another 4 hours. Use Perfection Spray and Mop Sauce once or twice more on the last hour of cooking.

7.   Rest the pork: Allow the meat to rest at room temperature for 2 hours, covered loosely.

8.   Carve and serve: Remove the bones from the pork butt and spoon the bark-like crust from the top of the meat. Slice or pull the meat and serve it with your favorite barbecue sauces.

Nutrition:

- **Energy (calories):** 189 kcal
- **Protein:** 14.55 g
- **Fat:** 9.09 g
- **Carbohydrates:** 13.21 g
- **Calcium:** 67 mg
- **Magnesium:** 40 mg
- **Phosphorus:** 163 mg
- **Iron:** 2 mg
- **Cholesterol:** 44 mg
- **Fiber:** 3 g
- **Sugars total:** 4.34 g
- **Starch:** 0.16 g

Smoke Lamb Recipes

10. Smoked Lamb Chops

Preparation time: 10 Minutes

Cooking time: 50 Minutes

Servings: 4

Ingredients:

- 1 rack of lamb, fat trimmed

- 2 tablespoons rosemary, fresh

- 2 tablespoons sage, fresh

- 1 tablespoon garlic cloves, roughly chopped

- 1/2 tablespoon salt

- 1/2 tablespoon pepper, coarsely ground

- 1/4 cup olive oil

- 1 tablespoon honey

Directions:

1.   Preheat your wood pellet smoker to 225 °F using a fruitwood.

2.   Put all your ingredients except the lamb in a food processor. Liberally apply the mixture to the lamb.

3.   Place the lamb on the smoker for 45 minutes or until the internal temperature reaches 120 °F.

4.   Sear the lamb on the grill for 2 minutes per side. Let rest for 5 minutes before serving.

Nutrition:

- **Energy (calories):** 545 kcal

- **Protein:** 52.02 g

- **Fat:** 35.22 g

- **Carbohydrates:** 6.34 g

- **Calcium:** 55 mg

- **Magnesium:** 62 mg

- **Phosphorus:** 470 mg

- **Iron:** 4.12 mg

11.   Wood Pellet smoked Lamb Shoulder

Preparation time: 10 minutes

Cooking time: 1hour 30 minutes

Servings: 7

Ingredients:

- 5-pounds lamb shoulder, boneless and excess fat trimmed

- 2 tablespoons kosher salt

- 2 tablespoons black pepper

- 1 tablespoon rosemary, dried

The Injection:

- 1 cup apple cider vinegar

The Spritz:

- 1 cup apple cider vinegar

- 1 cup apple juice

Directions:

1.   Smoke the wood pellet smoker with a water pan to 225 °F.

2.   Rinse the lamb in cold water then pat it dry with a paper towel. Inject vinegar into the lamb.

3.   Pat the lamb dries again and rub with oil, salt black pepper, and Rosemary. Tie with kitchen twine.

4.   Smoke uncovered for 1 hour then spritz after every 15 minutes until the internal temperature reaches 195 °F.

5.   Let cool before shredding it and enjoying it with your favorite side.

Nutrition:

- **Energy (calories):** 553 kcal

- **Protein:** 64.21 g

- **Fat:** 27.11 g

- **Carbohydrates:** 13.32 g

- **Calcium:** 58 mg

- **Magnesium:** 74 mg

- **Phosphorus:** 578 mg

- **Iron:** 3.98 mg

- **Cholesterol:** 181 mg

12.   Wood Pellet smoked Pulled Lamb Sliders

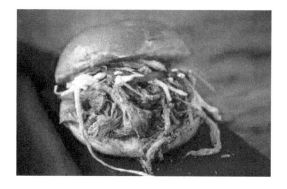

Preparation time: 10 minutes

Cooking time: 7 hours

Servings: 7

Ingredients:

For the Lamb's Shoulder:

- 5-pounds lamb shoulder, boneless

- 1/2 cup olive oil

- 1/4 cup dry rub

- 10 ounces spritz

- 1/3 cup kosher salt

- 1/3 cup pepper, ground

- 1-1/3 cup garlic, granulated

The Spritz:

- 4 ounces Worcestershire sauce

- 6 ounces apple cider vinegar

Directions:

1. Heat up a wood-burning smoker to 250 °F with a distilled water.

2. Clean some of the lamb's fat, then brush with oil and brush off.

3. For 90 minutes, put the lamb on the smoker and sprinkle with a spray bottle every 30 minutes until the temperature reached 165 °F.

4. Using the existing spritz liquid to move the lamb shoulder to a foil pan and cover securely with foil.

5. Put the smoker back in and fire until the heat within reaches 200 °F.

6. Start by removing from the smoker and leave to sit for 30 minutes and serve with slaw, bun, or aioli before removing the lamb. Enjoy it!

Nutrition:

- **Energy (calories):** 878 kcal

- **Protein:** 93.69 g

- **Fat:** 49.97 g

- **Carbohydrates:** 12.43 g

- **Calcium:** 99 mg

- **Magnesium:** 110 mg

- **Phosphorus:** 870 mg

- **Iron:** 7.47 mg

13. Savory smoked Lamb Leg with Green

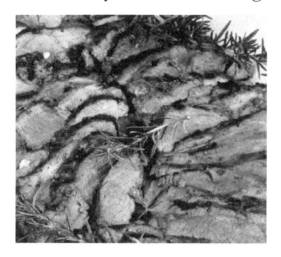

Preparation time: 6 hours

Cooking time: 5 Hours and 20 minutes

Servings: 10

Ingredients:

- Boneless lamb leg (4-lbs., 1.8-kg.)

The Rub:

- Minced garlic – 4 tablespoons

- Salt – 1 ½ tablespoon

- Ground black pepper – 1 tablespoon

- Oregano – 1 ½ tablespoon

- Thyme – 1 teaspoon

- Ginger – ½ teaspoon

- Canola oil – 3 tablespoons

The Salsa:

- Garlic – 4 cloves

- Diced onion – ¼ cup

- Green chili – 1 teaspoon

- Chopped fresh cilantro – ½ cup

- Sugar – ½ teaspoon

- Canola oil – 2 tablespoons

- Chicken broth – three-fourth cup

- Lemon juice – 2 tablespoons

Direction

1.   Cut the meat into 1-inch pieces and place them in a Ziploc bag. Add the rub ingredients to the Ziploc bag and close it. Shake the bag so that the spices thoroughly coat the meat. Refrigerate the bag overnight.

2.   Burn out all the wooden parts or use some other hotplate over a Traeger grill smoker. It is necessary to heat the smoke maker for about 2-3 hours. Place the meat on the bottom of the smoke maker and place fresh hickory wood chunks over the meat. Close the lid of the smoker and let the meat soak up the smoke for about one hour.

3.   Start to heat the grill at a medium-low temperature. Cook the meat on the grill using indirect heat for about five hours.

4.   Place the potatoes on the other rack.

5.   Add 3-4 tablespoons of canola oil to the lamb in a skillet. Add the salsa ingredients and cook the lamb over medium heat for about 10 minutes. Transfer the lamb to a platter and serve it along with the steak.

Nutrition:

- **Energy (calories):** 213 kcal
- **Protein:** 21.09 g
- **Fat:** 12.74 g
- **Carbohydrates:** 2.84 g
- **Calcium:** 23 mg
- **Magnesium:** 26 mg
- **Phosphorus:** 207 mg
- **Iron:** 1.95 mg

Smoked Poultry Recipes

14. Smoked Cornish Chicken in Wood Pellets

Preparation time: 0 minutes

Cooking time: 1 hour

Servings: 6

Ingredients:

- Cornish hens - 6

- Canola or avocado oil - 2-3 tbsp.

- Spice mix - 6 tbsp.

Directions:

1. Preheat your pellet grill to 285 Fahrenheit

2. Remove hens from packaging and pat dry with a paper towel.

3. Toss hens with oil so that both sides are coated. In a spice

blender, grind spices so that they resemble a paste.

4. Toss hens a second time and transfers to a smoker bag. Place smokie bags on the lowest rack and close grill lid. Let smoke for one hour.

5. If the temperature rises above 285 °F, turn off the main burner, and reduce the inbuilt fan.

Nutrition:

- **Energy (calories):** 850 kcal

- **Protein:** 100.2 g - **Fat:** 46.98 g

- **Carbohydrates:** 0.58 g

- **Calcium:** 60 mg

- **Magnesium:** 105 mg

- **Phosphorus:** 800 mg

- **Iron:** 3.7 mg

- **Sodium:** 165

15.   Wild Turkey Egg Rolls

Preparation time: 0 minutes

Cooking time: 40 minutes

Servings: 4-6

Ingredients:

- Corn one-half cup

- Leftover wild turkey meat - 2 cups

- Black beans one-half cup

- Taco seasoning 3 tbsp.

- Water one-half cup

- Rotel chilies and tomatoes - 1 can

- Egg roll wrappers 12

- Cloves of minced garlic 4

- 1 chopped Poblano pepper

- Chopped white onion one-half cup

Directions:

1.   In a bowl combine corn, turkey, beans, and taco seasoning. In a saucepan combine water, Rotel tomatoes and onions, and garlic. Heat until sauce heats.

2.   In a separate bowl, place 12 moist egg roll wrappers. Once the rolls have been filled - wrap them and make sure the seams face down.

3.   Warm a frying pan over medium heat and fry for 40 minutes on each side, or until golden brown.

4.   Serve with your favorite dipping sauce.

Nutrition:

- **Energy (calories):** 460 kcal

- **Protein:** 21.42 g

- **Fat:** 4.47 g

- **Carbohydrates:** 81.59 g

- **Calcium:** 73 mg

- **Magnesium:** 69 mg

- **Phosphorus:** 228 mg

- **Iron:** 6.65 mg

- **Fiber:** 5.6 g

- **Sugars total:** 2.42 g

- **Cholesterol:** 19.8 mg

16. Hellfire Chicken Wings

Preparation time: 15 minutes

Cooking time: 40 minutes

Servings: 6

Ingredients:

- 3 pounds chicken wings, tips removed

- 2 tablespoons olive oil

For the Rub:

- 1 teaspoon onion powder

- 1 teaspoon salt

- 1 teaspoon garlic powder

- 1 tablespoon paprika

- 1 teaspoon black pepper

- 1 teaspoon celery seed

- 1 teaspoon cayenne pepper

- 2 teaspoons brown sugar

For the Sauce:

- 4 jalapeno peppers, sliced crosswise

- 8 tablespoons butter, unsalted

- 1/2 cup hot sauce

- 1/2 cup cilantro leaves

Directions:

1.   Preheat oven to 375 degrees. Cut wings at joints and drop into a baking dish.

2.   Mix the remaining ingredients and rub over the wings - don't forget to rub the inside of the cavity as well.

3.   Bake for 35 minutes until the wings are opaque and the skin is beginning to crisp.

4.   To make the sauce, grill jalapeno peppers for 8 minutes on a gas grill or 3 minutes on an electric grill. Place jalapenos, butter, hot sauce, and cilantro into the bowl of a food processor and pulse until combined and smooth.

5.　　Heat sauce in a saucepan over medium heat for 8 minutes, stirring occasionally until it reaches your desired consistency and you can easily spoon it from the pan.

6.　　Make a small pile of chicken wings in the center of each plate and pour some sauce over the top!

Nutrition:

- **Energy (calories):** 482 kcal
- **Protein:** 50.64 g - **Fat:** 28.3 g
- **Carbohydrates:** 4.43 g
- **Calcium:** 52 mg
- **Magnesium:** 59 mg
- **Phosphorus:** 372 mg
- **Iron:** 2.68 mg
- **Cholesterol:** 170 mg
- **Fiber:** 1 g

17.   Spicy BBQ Chicken

Preparation time: 8 hours and 10 minutes

Cooking time: 3 hours

Servings: 6

Ingredients:

- 1 whole chicken, cleaned

For the Marinade:

- 1 medium white onion, peeled

- 6 Thai chilies

- 5 cloves of garlic, peeled

- 1 scotch bonnet

- 3 tablespoons salt

- 2 tablespoons sugar

- 2 tablespoons sweet paprika

- 4 cups grapeseed oil

45

Directions:

1.   Put the chilies in a food processor and blend until smooth. Add this paste to a large bowl.

2.   Skin and debone the chicken, and add it to the large bowl. Add the paprika, sugar, and salt to the bowl. Stir until the chicken is well coated with the marinade. Fridge overnight.

3.   Preheat your smoker to 350F. Pour the grapeseed oil into a large oven-safe pan.

4.   Arrange the chicken in a single layer. Cook in the oven for about 3 hours, or until the chicken can be easily pierced with a fork.

5.   Serve with coleslaw and corn.

Nutrition:

- **Energy (calories):** 5045 kcal

- **Protein:** 296.93 g - **Fat:** 273.97 g

- **Carbohydrates:** 364.78 g

- **Calcium:** 892 mg

- **Magnesium:** 830 mg

- **Phosphorus:** 3348 mg

- **Iron:** 26.04 mg

- **Fiber:** 55.8 g

18. Teriyaki Wings

Preparation time: 8 hours

Cooking time: 50 minutes

Servings: 8

Ingredients:

- 2 and one-half pounds large chicken wings

- 1 tablespoon toasted sesame seeds

For the Marinade:

- 2 scallions, sliced

- 2 tablespoons grated ginger

- One-half teaspoon minced garlic

- 1/4 cup brown sugar

- 1/2 cup soy sauce

- 2 tablespoons rice wine vinegar

47

- 2 teaspoons sesame oil
- 1/4 cup water

Directions:

1. Soak 2 cups of wood chips in water for 30 minutes. Preheat oven to 375 degrees Fahrenheit.

2. Cut small slits in the chicken wings and put them in a large bowl. Mix in 1 tablespoon sesame seeds.

3. Process the marinade ingredients in a blender. Pour into the waiting bowl with the chicken wings and sesame seeds. Stir and let stand at room temperature for 8 hours.

4. Prepare the grill for indirect cooking. Do not soak the wood chips. Stand the chicken wings in a foil roasting pan or a baking sheet.

5. Bake the wings at 375 degrees Fahrenheit for 50 minutes.

6. Grill the wings over low heat. Shake the wings after 3 minutes until thoroughly heated.

Nutrition:

- **Energy (calories):** 331 kcal
- **Protein:** 23.73 g
- **Fat:** 18.88 g
- **Carbohydrates:** 15.39 g
- **Calcium:** 47 mg
- **Magnesium:** 37 mg
- **Phosphorus:** 262 mg
- **Iron:** 3.1 mg

19.   Kansas City hot Fried Chicken

Preparation time: 1 hour

Cooking time: 25 minutes

Servings: 4

Ingredients:

- 1 whole chicken, cut into pieces

- 3/2 cup buttermilk

- 2 tablespoons hot sauce

- 4 cups All-Purpose flour

- 1 teaspoon salt

- 1/2 teaspoon black pepper

- 1/2 Tablespoon red pepper flakes

- 12 ounces bacon, uncooked, chopped

- As needed vegetable oil

Direction:

1.   Prepare frying station by placing over medium heat: 3-quart cast iron pot, spritz bottle with vegetable oil, wire rack set in a rimmed baking sheet.

2.   Mix 3-4 cups vegetable oil and hot sauce in a pot.

3.   Mix buttermilk, flour, and salt in a large bowl.

4.   Pat chicken dry. Sprinkle with pepper. Dip chicken into buttermilk mixture then dredges in flour mixture. Set aside on a wire rack.

5.   Fry chicken in batches until golden brown and internal temperature reaches 165 degrees F. Transfer to plate lined with paper towels.

6.   Cook bacon in a nonstick skillet over medium-high heat; transfer to paper towels.

7.   Put bacon, chicken, hot sauce, and red pepper flakes into a cast-iron skillet. Turn to coat. Serve.

Nutrition:

- **Energy (calories):** 909 kcal
- **Protein:** 69.76 g
- **Fat:** 22.67 g
- **Carbohydrates:** 103.74 g
- **Calcium:** 165 mg
- **Magnesium:** 104 mg
- **Phosphorus:** 727 mg
- **Iron:** 9.54 mg

20.   Clucky Kentucky hot brown Casserole

Preparation time: 10 minutes

Cooking time: 40 minutes

Servings: 8-10

Ingredients:

- One-fourth cup butter

- One-fourth cup flour

- 4 cups of milk

- 1 egg

- 1 cup fresh grated parmesan cheese

- One-half teaspoon salt

- 1 teaspoon coarse ground black pepper

- 1 teaspoon granulated garlic

- 1 teaspoon smoked paprika

- 12 slices white or sourdough bread, toasted and cubed

- 1½ pounds cooked, smoked chicken, either shredded or sliced thin

- ½ pound bacon

- 1 cup heirloom tomato, sliced

- ½ cup parmesan cheese

- ¼ cup fresh parsley, chopped

Directions:

1. Preheat oven to 350 °F.

2. Heat ¼ cup butter in a large pot over medium-high heat.

3. Add flour and cook until lightly browned about 1-2 minutes.

4. Whisk in milk and simmer until thickened, about 8 minutes.

5. Whisk in remaining ingredients, except chicken, bacon, tomato, parsley, and parmesan cheese.

6. Simmer mixture, stirring occasionally, until it thickens, about 5-7 minutes.

7. Add chicken, bacon, and tomatoes. Remove from heat.

8. Pour mixture into a greased 9x13" casserole dish. Top with parmesan cheese and parsley.

9. Bake uncovered in the preheated oven until golden brown, about 40 minutes. Serve hot.

Nutrition:

- **Energy (calories):** 886 kcal
- **Protein:** 30.42 g - **Fat:** 66.28 g
- **Carbohydrates:** 43.59 g
- **Calcium:** 370 mg
- **Magnesium:** 51 mg
- **Phosphorus:** 411 mg
- **Iron:** 4.71 mg

Extra Smoke Recipes

21.   Goat Chops

Preparation time: 5 minutes

Cooking time: 8 minutes

Servings: 8

Ingredients:

* 8 1-inch thick goat chops

Marinade:

* 6 garlic cloves (minced)

* 1 tbsp. dried oregano

* One-fourth tsp salt

* 1 tsp ground black pepper

* One-half cup dry white wine

* 1 lemon (juiced)

- 1 tbsp. grated lemon zest
- 1 onion (chopped)

Directions:

1. Combine all the marinade ingredients in a mixing bowl. Add the goat chops and toss to combine. Leave the goat chops in the marinade for about 30 minutes.

2. Start the grill on smoke mode, leaving the lid open for 5 minutes for the fire to start.

3. Close the lid and preheat the grill to "high," with the lid closed for 15 minutes.

4. Place the goat chops on the grill grate and smoke for 8 minutes, 4 minutes per side.

5. Remove goat chops from heat and let it cool for a few minutes.

6. Serve.

Nutrition:

- **Energy (calories):** 535 kcal
- **Protein:** 95.54 g
- **Fat:** 12.03 g
- **Carbohydrates:** 5.07 g
- **Calcium:** 113 mg
- **Magnesium:** 8 mg
- **Phosphorus:** 863 mg
- **Iron:** 13.07 mg
- **Fiber:** 0.5 g

22.   Smoked Goose Breast

Preparation time: 15 minutes

Cooking time: 45 minutes

Servings: 8

Ingredients:

- 8 goose breasts

Marinade:

- 4 tbsp. soy sauce

- 5 tbsp. brown sugar

- 4 tbsp. honey

- 1 tsp. garlic powder

- 1 tbsp. Dijon mustard

- 1/3 cup olive oil

- One-half cup pineapple juice

- 1 tsp. paprika

- One-half tsp cayenne pepper

Directions:

1. Mix together soy sauce, brown sugar, honey, garlic powder, and mustard.

2. Place goose breasts in a baking dish. Pour marinade over the goose, reserving 2 tbsp. of marinade for sauce.

3. Marinade for sauce. Reserve 1/3 of the marinade for sauce.

4. Marinate the goose breasts for 15 minutes.

5. Set aside pineapple juice. Mix with the rest of the marinade and paprika.

6. Heat the Traeger grill smoker.

7. Place breasts skin down in Smoker for 45 minutes.

8. Pour marinade over goose breasts. Cover the pan, and reduce heat to medium-low. Cook for 40 minutes. Rest for 5 minutes, then slice thinly. Drizzle with reserved sauce and pineapple juice.

Nutrition:

- **Energy (calories):** 991 kcal
- **Protein:** 155.26 g
- **Fat:** 36.01 g
- **Carbohydrates:** 13.46 g
- **Calcium:** 33 mg
- **Magnesium:** 193 mg
- **Phosphorus:** 1643 mg
- **Iron:** 37.9 mg
- **Potassium:** 2204 mg
- **Fiber:** 0.5 g

23.   Smoked Venison Tenderloin

Preparation time: 15 minutes

Cooking time: 2 hours

Servings: 4

Ingredients:

- 1-pound venison tenderloin or backstrap

- 1 tbsp. ground black pepper

- 2/3 cup olive oil

- 5 garlic cloves (minced)

- 1 tsp. dried thyme

- 1 tsp. dried oregano

- 1 tsp. paprika

- 1 tsp. freshly chopped peppermint

- 1 tbsp. kosher salt

- 1 cup balsamic vinegar

Directions:

1. Cut the tenderloin or backstrap and place it in a bowl. Add the ground pepper, thyme, oregano, paprika, peppermint, salt, and garlic; add the olive oil, and toss, fully coating the meat. Refrigerate for 1 to 2 hours.

2. After 1 to 2 hours, take the tenderloin out and place it on a hot smoker with the pepper and garlic. Cook it for 2 hours.

3. Next, add the balsamic, cover it with the lid, and reduce the heat.

4. Serve alongside wild rice and steamed vegetables.

Nutrition:

- **Energy (calories):** 558 kcal
- **Protein:** 34.8 g
- **Fat:** 38.97 g
- **Carbohydrates:** 13.71 g
- **Calcium:** 40 mg
- **Magnesium:** 51 mg
- **Phosphorus:** 365 mg
- **Iron:** 5.95 mg

24.   Smoked Rabbit

Preparation time: 15 minutes

Cooking time: 3 hours

Servings: 4

Ingredients:

- 1 (3 pounds) whole rabbit

- 1 tbsp. dried rosemary

- 1/3 cup olive oil

- 1 tbsp. dried thyme

- 1 tbsp. cracked black pepper

- 1 tsp. sea salt

- One-half cup dry white wine

- 1 cup apple juice

- 1 tbsp. dried oregano

- 1 tbsp. freshly grated lemon zest

Directions:

1.   Rinse and pat dry the rabbit. Cover it with the dried rosemary, olive oil, thyme, black pepper, and sea salt, making sure the entire rabbit is coated.

2. Cover the rabbit with plastic wrap and place it in the refrigerator.

3. Consume within two to three days. Thaw overnight and refrigerate for 8 hours. Season the rabbit with the white wine, apple juice, oregano, and lemon zest.

4. Cover with a layer of plastic wrap and refrigerate overnight. Heat up your barbecue/smoking machine to medium heat. Place the rabbit on the smoker. Smoke it for three hours, or until the liquid in the pan reduces by three quarters.

5. Check every hour to baste the rabbit with the reduced liquid. When finished, remove from the smoker and let the rabbit cool down. Slice to serve.

Nutrition:

- **Energy (calories):** 301 kcal

- **Protein:** 6.85 g

- **Fat:** 24.64 g

- **Carbohydrates:** 14.3 g

- **Calcium:** 225 mg

- **Magnesium:** 22 mg

- **Phosphorus:** 161 mg

- **Iron:** 0.54 mg

- **Fiber:** 0.7 g

25. Spatchcock smoked Quail

Preparation time: 15 minutes

Cooking time: 1 hour

Servings: 4

Ingredients:

- 4 quails

- 2 tbsp. finely chopped fresh parsley

- 1 tbsp. finely chopped fresh rosemary

- 2 tbsp. finely chopped fresh thyme

- One-half cup melted butter

- 1 tsp. garlic powder

- 1 tsp. onion powder

- 1 tsp. ground black pepper

- 2 tsp. salt or to taste

- 2 tbsp. finely chopped scallions

Directions:

1.   Remove the giblets from the quail; set aside. Rinse the quails under cold running water, and pat dry with paper towels. Prepare the grill for cooking; place the quail on the grill rack, and brush them with butter. Cook about 1 hour, brushing with melted butter every 5 minutes, until evenly brown.

2.   The internal temperature should reach 170 deg. F. Meanwhile, prepare a marinade by combining the fresh herbs, scallions, garlic, onion powders, salt, ground black pepper, and salt; mix well.

3.   Prepare the quail; pour the marinade over the quail, and place them in a glass baking dish, seam-side down. Cover with plastic wrap, and refrigerate overnight.

4.   Serve with mashed potatoes and roasted vegetables.

Nutrition:

- **Energy (calories):** 339 kcal
- **Protein:** 20.87 g
- **Fat:** 27.28 g
- **Carbohydrates:** 2.84 g
- **Calcium:** 35 mg
- **Magnesium:** 32 mg
- **Phosphorus:** 303 mg
- **Iron:** 4.77 mg
- **Fiber:** 0.7 g

26.   Smoked Pheasant

Preparation time: 15 minutes

Cooking time: 5 hours

Servings: 5

Ingredients:

- 2 whole pheasants

- 4 tbsp. brown sugar

- 1 tbsp. kosher salt

- 1 tbsp. black peppercorns

- 4 cups of water

- 2 cups maple syrup

- 1 cup pineapple juice

- 1 tbsp. Dijon mustard

Directions:

1.   Rinse pheasant, pat dry. Rub all over with brown sugar, salt & pepper.

2.   Place 4 cups water in the bottom of a pot with high sides. Place pheasants in a pot, bring to a boil for 20-30 minutes. Turn off the heat, drain off the liquid through a strainer. Pat dry.

3.   Place breast-side up on a rack inside a roasting pan, with the rack sitting in low boiling water. Spoon on maple syrup, pineapple juice & mustard.

4.   Cover with foil. Roast for 4 hours at 250 °F, basting regularly with the juices in the pan. Remove foil and roast for 4 hours more, basting whenever possible. Enjoy it!

Nutrition:

- **Energy (calories):** 735 kcal

- **Protein:** 66.77 g - **Fat:** 10.48 g

- **Carbohydrates:** 92.69 g

- **Calcium:** 195 mg

- **Magnesium:** 95 mg

- **Phosphorus:** 657 mg

- **Iron:** 3.6 mg

- **Fiber:** 0.5 g

- **Sugars total:** 83.52 g

27.   Rabbit Stew

Preparation time: 15 minutes

Cooking time: 2 hours and 30 minutes

Servings: 4

Ingredients:

- 1 (3 pounds) rabbit (cut into bite sizes)

- One-fourth cup olive oil

- 1 medium onion (chopped)

- 1 carrot (diced)

- 1 stalk celery (diced)

- 2 roman tomato (sliced)

- 1 red bell pepper (sliced)

- 2 garlic cloves (minced)

- 1 cup red wine

- 4 cups chicken broth

- 2 bay leaves

- 2 tbsp. flour

- 1 tsp. dried thyme

- 1 tsp. salt

- 1 tsp. ground black pepper

Directions:

1. Prepare your grilling machine.

2. In a large pot over medium heat, add in olive oil and heat. Sauté onion, celery, carrot, red bell pepper, and garlic for 2 minutes, stirring constantly.

3. Add in rabbit pieces, red wine, dried thyme, bay leaves, salt, & ground black pepper. Stir to coat rabbit. Add in enough broth so that rabbit is submerged, then cover.

4. Bring to a boil then turn heat to low. Simmer for at least 2 hours. Check occasionally to make sure the rabbit is submerged and that there is adequate liquid.

5. Mix together 4 tbsp. flour and 1 cup of broth. Slowly stir into the rabbit.

6. Continue cooking on low heat uncovered for 30 minutes until the rabbit is tender.

Nutrition:

- **Energy (calories):** 1112 kcal

- **Protein:** 54.24 g

- **Fat:** 45.03 g

- **Carbohydrates:** 116.63 g

- **Calcium:** 58 mg

- **Magnesium:** 62 mg

- **Phosphorus:** 373 mg

- **Iron:** 3.72 mg

- **Fiber:** 2.1 g

Smoked Fish and Seafood Recipes

28. Grilled Teriyaki Salmon

Preparation time: 10 minutes

Cooking time: 30 minutes

Serves: 4

Ingredients:

- 1 salmon fillet
- 1/8 cup olive oil
- 1/2 tbsp. salt
- 1/4 tbsp. pepper
- 1/4 tbsp. garlic salt

- 1/4 cup butter, sliced
- 1/4 teriyaki sauce
- 1 tbsp. sesame seeds

Direction:

1. Preheat the grill to 400 °F.

2. Place the salmon fillet on a non-stick foil sheet. Drizzle the salmon with oil, seasonings, and butter on top.

3. Pace the foil tray on the grill and close the lid. Cook for 8 minutes then open the lid.

4. Brush the salmon with teriyaki sauce and repeat after every 5 minutes until all sauce is finished.

5. Serve and enjoy with your favorite side dish.

Nutrition:

- **Energy (calories):** 561 kcal
- **Protein:** 52.19 g
- **Fat:** 37.7 g
- **Carbohydrates:** 0.68 g
- **Calcium:** 502 mg
- **Magnesium:** 83 mg
- **Phosphorus:** 821 mg
- **Iron:** 1.64 mg
- **Fiber:** 0 g

29. Wood Pellet Togarashi Grilled Salmon

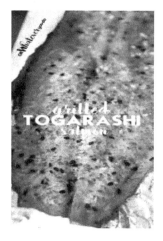

Preparation time: 5 minutes

Cooking time: 20 minutes

Serves: 6

Ingredients:

- 1 salmon fillet

- 1/4 cup olive oil

- 1/2 tbsp. kosher salt

- 1 tbsp. Togarashi seasoning

Direction:

1.   Preheat your smoker to 400 °F.

2.   Place the salmon fillet on a non-stick foil sheet with the skin side up.

3.   Rub the olive oil on the salmon and sprinkle with salt and togarashi seasoning.

4.   Place the salmon on the preheated grill and close the lid. Cook for 20 minutes or until the internal temperature reaches 145 °F.

5.   Serve when hot. Enjoy i!.

Nutrition:

- **Energy (calories):** 561 kcal
- **Protein:** 0.06 g
- **Fat:** 9 g
- **Carbohydrates:** 0.83 g
- **Calcium:** 0 mg
- **Magnesium:** 0 mg
- **Phosphorus:** 0 mg
- **Iron:** 0.16 mg
- **Fiber:** 0 g

30.   Grilled Lingcod

Preparation time: 10 minutes

Cooking time: 15 minutes

Serves: 6

Ingredients:

- 2 lb. lingcod fillets
- 1/2 tbsp. salt
- 1/2 tbsp. white pepper
- 1/4 tbsp. cayenne
- Lemon wedges

Direction:

1.   Start firing up the wood pellet grill to 375 °F.

2.   Place the lingcod on parchment paper and season it with salt, white pepper, cayenne pepper then tops with the lemon.

3.   Place the fish on the grill and cook for 15 minutes or until the internal temperature reaches 145°F.

4.   Serve and enjoy it!

Nutrition:

- **Energy (calories):** 133 kcal

- **Protein:** 26.82 g

- **Fat:** 1.67 g

- **Carbohydrates:** 1.09 g

- **Calcium:** 24 mg

- **Magnesium:** 41 mg

- **Phosphorus:** 306 mg

- **Iron:** 0.6 mg

- **Sodium:** 442 mg

31. Wood Pellet Rockfish

Preparation time: 10 minutes

Cooking time: 20 minutes

Serves: 6

Ingredients:

- 6 rockfish fillets

- 1 lemon, sliced

- 3/4 tbsp. Himalayan salt

- 2 tbsp. fresh dill, chopped

- 1/2 tbsp. garlic powder

- 1/2 tbsp. onion powder

- 6 tbsp. butter

Direction:

1.   Heat up your smoker to 375 °F.

2.   Place the rockfish in a baking dish and season with salt, dill, garlic, and onion.

3.   Place butter on top of the fish then closes it. Cook for 20 minutes or until the fish is no longer translucent.

4.   Remove from grill and let sit for 5 minutes before serving. Enjoy it!

Nutrition:

- **Energy (calories):** 287 kcal

- **Protein:** 35.76 g - **Fat:** 14.43 g

- **Carbohydrates:** 2.83 g

- **Calcium:** 67 mg

- **Magnesium:** 59 mg

- **Phosphorus:** 407 mg

- **Iron:** 1.02 mg

- **Potassium:** 791 mg

- **Sodium:** 381 mg

32. Salt and Pepper Spot Prawn Skewer

Preparation time: 10 minutes

Cooking time: 10 minutes

Serves: 6

Ingredients:

- 2 lb. spot prawns, clean

- 2 tbsp. oil

- Salt and pepper to taste

Direction:

1. Preheat your grill to 400 °F.

2. Meanwhile, soak the skewers then skewer with the prawns.

3. Brush with oil then season with salt and pepper to taste.

4. Place the skewers in the grill, and cook for 5 minutes on each side.

5. Serve and Enjoy it!

Nutrition:

- **Energy (calories):** 229 kcal
- **Protein:** 28.14 g
- **Fat:** 11.96 g
- **Carbohydrates:** 0.71 g
- **Calcium:** 23 mg
- **Magnesium:** 65 mg
- **Phosphorus:** 285 mg
- **Iron:** 0.58 mg
- **Sugar:** 0 g

33. Bacon-Wrapped Scallops

Preparation time: 15 minutes

Cooking time: 20 minutes

Serves: 8

Ingredients:

- 1 lb. sea scallops

- 1/2 lb. bacon

- Salt to taste

Direction:

1.   Preheat your grill to 375 °F.

2.   Pat dry the scallops with a paper towel then wrap with the bacon and secure with a toothpick.

3.   Lay the scallops on the grill with the bacon side down. Cook for 7 minutes on each side.

4.   The bacon should be crispy and scallops tender. Serve and enjoy it!

Nutrition:

- **Energy (calories):** 151 kcal

- **Protein:** 14.67 g

- **Fat:** 8.85 g

- **Carbohydrates:** 4.86 g

- **Calcium:** 12 mg

- **Magnesium:** 26 mg

- **Phosphorus:** 261 mg

- **Iron:** 1.01 mg

- **Sugar:** 0 g

Smoked Vegetable Recipes

34.   Smoked Hummus

Preparation time: 15 minutes

Cooking time: 20 minutes

Serving: 6

Ingredients:

- 1 and one-half cups chickpeas, rinsed and drained

- One-fourth cup tahini

- 1 tablespoon garlic, minced

- 2 tablespoons extra virgin olive oil

- 1 teaspoon salt

- 4 tablespoons lemon juice

Direction

1.   Make the fire to 350 °F for 15 minutes with your best wood pellet

2.   Spread the chickpeas on a sheet tray and place it on the grill grate. Smoke for 20 minutes.

3.   Let the chickpeas cool at room temperature.

4.   Place smoked chickpeas in a blender or food processor. Add in the rest of the ingredients. Pulse until smooth.

5.   Serve with roasted vegetables if desired.

Nutrition:

- **Energy (calories):** 295 kcal

- **Protein:** 8.73 g

- **Fat:** 24.16 g

- **Carbohydrates:** 15.44 g

- **Calcium:** 185 mg

- **Magnesium:** 45 mg

- **Phosphorus:** 317 mg

- **Iron:** 3.86 mg

35. Grilled Corn on the Cob with Parmesan and Garlic

Preparation time: 15 minutes

Cooking time: 20 minutes

Serving: 6

Ingredients:

- 4 tablespoons butter, melted

- 2 cloves of garlic, minced

- Salt and pepper to taste

- 8 corns, unhusked

- One half cup parmesan cheese, grated

- 1 tablespoon parsley chopped

Direction

1.   Fire your new Traeger Grill to 450 °F. Close the smoker and preheat for 15 minutes.

2.   Place butter, garlic, salt, and pepper in a bowl and mix until well combined.

3.   Peel the corn husk but do not detach the husk from the corn. Remove the silk. Brush the corn with the garlic butter mixture and close the husks.

4.   Place the corn on the grill grate and cook for 30 minutes turning the corn every 5 minutes for even cooking.

Nutrition:

- **Energy (calories):** 2302 kcal

- **Protein:** 58.95 g

- **Fat:** 38.04 g

- **Carbohydrates:** 450.32 g

- **Calcium:** 141 mg

- **Magnesium:** 774 mg

- **Phosphorus:** 1338 mg

- **Iron:** 16.61 mg

36. Grilled Asparagus with Wild Mushrooms

Preparation time: 15 minutes

Cooking time: 10 minutes

Serving: 4

Ingredients:

- 2 bunches fresh asparagus, trimmed

- 4 cups wild mushrooms, sliced

- 1 large shallot, sliced into rings

- Extra virgin oil as needed

- 2 tablespoons butter, melted

Direction:

1.   Light up your Traeger grill Smoker to 500 °F. Preheat for 15 minutes.

2.   Place the asparagus, mushrooms, and shallots on a baking tray. Drizzle with oil and butter and season with salt and pepper to taste.

3.   Place on a baking tray and cook for 10 minutes. Make sure to give the asparagus a good stir halfway through the cooking time for even browning.

Nutrition:

- **Energy (calories):** 654 kcal
- **Protein:** 23.81 g - **Fat:** 10.9 g
- **Carbohydrates:** 120.2 g
- **Calcium:** 37 mg
- **Magnesium:** 285 mg
- **Phosphorus:** 699 mg
- **Iron:** 3.31 mg

37.   Grilled Scallions

Preparation time: 15 minutes

Cooking time: 10 minutes

Serving: 4

Ingredients:

- 10 whole scallions, chopped

- One-fourth cup olive oil

- Salt and pepper to taste

- 2 tablespoons rice vinegar

- 1 whole jalapeno, sliced into rings

Direction:

1.   Put fire to 4500F for 15 minutes.

2.   Place on a bowl all ingredients and toss to coat. Transfer to a parchment-lined baking tray.

3.   Serve on the grill grate and grill for 20 minutes.

Nutrition:

- **Energy (calories):** 228 kcal
- **Protein:** 1.13 g - **Fat:** 23.3 g
- **Carbohydrates:** 3.9 g
- **Calcium:** 30 mg
- **Magnesium:** 12 mg
- **Phosphorus:** 29 mg
- **Iron:** 0.7 mg
- **Sugar:** 4.6 g

38. Rosemary and Thyme-Infused Mashes Potatoes with Cream

Preparation time: 20 minutes

Cooking time: 1 hour

Servings: 6

Ingredients:

- Pound russet potatoes
- Cup water
- Pint heavy cream
- 2 Rosemary sprigs
- 3 thyme sprigs
- 2 tablespoons thyme leaves
- 6 sage, Leaves
- 6 peppercorns

- 2 garlics

- 2 butter, Sticks

- To taste salt

- To taste ground black pepper

Direction:

1. In a small saucepan, bring the water, butter, garlic, thyme, and rosemary to a simmer over low heat. Cover the pan and simmer for 30 minutes. Strain the herb from the mixture, discard the rosemary and return the liquid back to a simmer.

2. While the liquid is simmering, cut the potatoes into 1/2 slices and cut the pieces into bite-sized pieces (about 2-3 bites). Add the hot herb-y liquid to the potatoes and combine well. Cover with a tight-fitting lid and turn the heat down to low, and simmer until the potatoes are tender.

3. Add the heavy cream and continue to simmer uncovered for 5 minutes more (or until the cream has thickened slightly). The cream will let the potatoes soak up its flavors, making the taste more favorable.

4. In a sauté pan, add the remaining thyme, sage, rosemary, garlic, butter and bring to a simmer.

5. Remove from the heat, cover, and press the leaves of the fresh herbs into the softened butter with a fork. Mash the herbs a bit to release their essence.

6.   Add 1/2 the herb butter to the potatoes, season the potatoes to taste with salt and ground black pepper, and mash in the herb butter to create a chunky consistency.

7.   You can serve the cooked potatoes immediately, warm, or at room temperature.

Nutrition:

- **Energy (calories):** 424 kcal
- **Protein:** 7.16 g - **Fat:** 30.95 g
- **Carbohydrates:** 39.49 g
- **Calcium:** 673 mg
- **Magnesium:** 196 mg
- **Phosphorus:** 114 mg
- **Iron:** 3.86 mg

39.   Mashed Red Potatoes

Preparation time: 15 minutes

Cooking time: 40 minutes

Servings: 4

Ingredients:

- 8 large red potatoes

- To taste salt

- To taste black pepper

- 1/2 cup heavy cream

- 1/4 cup butter

- To taste salt

- To taste black pepper

Direction:

1.   Wash and peel the red potatoes, then dice them into cubes. Remember to wash your hands and dry them with a towel after handling the potatoes.

2.   Place potatoes in the pan with enough cold water to fully cover the potatoes, add 1/2 teaspoon salt to the pan or enough salt to taste when you consume the potatoes later.

3.   Boil the potatoes over medium heat until tender. Stir occasionally to prevent them from sticking to the bottom. To test for doneness, stick a fork or knife in the potato cubes. If they go through smoothly, they are ready. If not, cook them longer until they are slightly firm.

4.   Drain the potatoes and allow them to cool slightly for a couple of minutes, keeping in mind that you will burn your mouth if you eat them right out of the stove.

5.   Put the potatoes through a potato ricer or mash them up by hand carefully, or you can use a food processor and mix the potatoes for about 10 seconds.

6.   Put a saucepan on medium heat. Add butter and cream and bring it to a simmer. Add potatoes to the pan and mix well.

7.   Add salt and pepper to taste. Serve immediately.

Nutrition:

- **Energy (calories):** 679 kcal
- **Protein:** 14.83 g
- **Fat:** 18.15 g
- **Carbohydrates:** 119.9 g
- **Calcium:** 91 mg
- **Magnesium:** 169 mg
- **Phosphorus:** 473 mg
- **Iron:** 5.66 mg

40.   Baked Sweet Potato Casserole with Marshmallow Fluff

Preparation time: 10 minutes

Cooking time: 1 hour

Servings: 6

Ingredients:

- 3 Pound sweet potatoes

- 1/2 cup milk

- 1/3 cup brown sugar

- 3 eggs

- 4 Tablespoon butter

- 1/2 teaspoon salt

- 3 egg white

- 333/500 Cup brown sugar

- 1 Pinch salt

- 1 Pinch ground cinnamon

Direction:

1.   Place potatoes in the oven; cook at 325 degrees for 1 hour or until done.

2.   Extract the sweet potatoes from the oven. Take the skins off the potatoes and mash them in a bowl.

3.   Add brown sugar and milk. Mix until blended. Add egg and mix well.

4.   Stir in the butter and salt. Place mixture into a greased casserole dish.

5.   In a mixing bowl, beat 3 egg whites with brown sugar. Mix in salt, cinnamon, and bread crumbs. Spread topping over the potato mixture.

6.   Bake at 350 degrees for 30 minutes.

Nutrition:

- **Energy (calories):** 679 kcal

- **Protein:** 14.83 g - **Fat:** 18.15 g

- **Carbohydrates:** 119.9 g

- **Calcium:** 91 mg

- **Magnesium:** 169 mg

- **Phosphorus:** 473 mg

- **Iron:** 5.66 mg

41. Baked Garlic Duchess Potatoes

Preparation time: 30 minutes

Cooking time: 1 hour

Servings: 8

Ingredients:

- 12 medium Yukon Gold potatoes

- To taste salt

- 5 large egg yolk

- 2 cloves garlic, minced

- 31/25 cups heavy cream

- 3/1 cup sour cream

- 10 tablespoons butter, melted

- To taste black pepper

Direction:

1.   Cook potatoes in a pot of boiling water for 10 minutes, skins on. Drain.

2.   Do not remove skins at this stage. Place potatoes back into the hot pot. Cover again with boiling water and cook about 10 minutes or until fork tender (to test, insert a fork into a potato and twist it easily.) Remove from water and drain.

3.   Bring cream, sour cream, and butter to a simmer over medium-high heat. Stir to combine. Turn off the burner. Mix in potatoes, salt, and pepper. Transfer mixture into greased pan (8 x 11 casserole is best). Pierce tops of potatoes with a fork making evenly spaced holes. Gently press garlic into each hole. Bake at 450° for 1 hour. (Longer if desired) Remove from the oven and let it cool at least an hour before serving.

Nutrition:

- **Energy (calories):** 685 kcal
- **Protein:** 14.31 g - **Fat:** 26.9 g
- **Carbohydrates:** 99.92 g
- **Calcium:** 129 mg
- **Magnesium:** 133 mg
- **Phosphorus:** 392 mg
- **Iron:** 4.71 mg

•

Conclusion

Congratulations on making it to the end of this book. Grilling is one of the most popular cooking processes that guarantee a perfect taste to your recipes. Grilling is a much healthier method than others because it benefits food, preserves flavor and nutrients. But on the other hand, a Traeger grill smoker wood pellet grill allows you to grill your food quickly and with less effort and smoke. The advantage of having a Traeger grill smoker in your home is versatility, it helps you cook food faster, provides a temperature monitoring scale and is one of the essential parts of cooking. and I hope you will be satisfied.

Enjoy.

CPSIA information can be obtained
at www.ICGtesting.com
Printed in the USA
BVHW091058030521
606332BV00004B/458